THE BALLAD OF

ROBIN HOOD

From Sherwood Forest dark
and eerie
Comes a story often told
Of the outlaw Robin Hood
And his men so brave and bold.

Through the woods they crept
at midnight
Stalking unsuspecting prey.
To the poor they gave the gold
Taken from the rich each day.

Enemies they had aplenty –
All the rich who ruled the land
Who had sworn to kill the outlaw
And the members of his band.

But the peasants poor and lowly
Sang his praises loud and clear
By their hearths in homes
so humble
Never for the Sheriff's ear.

ROBIN MEETS LITTLE JOHN

While hunting in the leafy
greenwood
Robin came upon a man
Looking large, uncompromising
Between them both the water ran.

They stepped on the bridge
together
And the stranger he did roar
"Make way, you little woodsman
Or my staff will make you sore."

Robin laughed and said,
"You're welcome
I will use a staff as well."
But his opponent swiped
him cleanly.
Into the stream he duly fell.

"I'm John Little at your service,"
Said the giant with a smile.
"I'm Robin Hood," replied the loser
"Will you join my band awhile?"

ROBIN MEETS FRIAR TUCK

One day down beside a river
When its waters were in flood
Robin wondered how he'd cross
Keeping dry and clear
of mud.

Then he spied a friar fishing.
Smiling to himself he said,
"Carry me across the water
If you don't, you're surely dead."

The friar shrugged his shoulders slowly.

"Climb upon my back," said he.

Into the water he tossed Robin.

"Who are you to order me?"

"I'm Robin Hood, the outlaw leader.
We need a churchman just like you.
Come and join us in the greenwood
Where you'll find the men all true."

Now Robin's band had grown
to many.
Little John and Friar Tuck
Much the Miller and Will Stukely
Were a few who brought him luck.

Robin met a wandering minstrel
Looking sad, in deep despair,
"My dear love's to wed an
old man.
To marry him she does not care."

Robin gathered all his comrades,
"To the church we must attend."
They caught the old man
and the bishop
Before the wedding march could end.

The Friar joined the two young
lovers,
Alan and his Alice fair
And they sped into the forest
To find a longed-for refuge there.

Hunting late was William Stukely
When he heard a frightened moan.
In a trap a youth was crying,
"My brother's young and home alone."

Will left the lad safe with the outlaws
Went to town the child to find.
The child assured, homeward returning
Will was captured, his death signed.

The outlaws moved to save their
comrade
With news of the hangman's rope.
In disguise they reached the scaffold.
Little John brought Will his hope.

Acting as a saddened kinsman
John embraced the condemned man.
He cut the bonds
they leapt to freedom
Fleeing to the woods they ran.

ROBIN WEDS MARION

When Robin was a bright
young fellow
He grew to love a maiden free.
He left her lonely and forsaken
When to the greenwood he did flee.

Maiden Marion was that lady.
Now her father wished her wed.
He chose a rich and evil
bridegroom
So to Sherwood she, too, fled.

Marion dressed up as a peasant
Was mistaken for a boy.
Robin fought him, found 'twas Marion
Then his heart was full of joy.

There was a wedding bright and
cheerful
In the forest green that day.
Friar Tuck he led the service.
Alan a Dale his lute did play.

ROBIN'S CAPTURE

While King Richard was
crusading
His young brother, bad Prince John
Declared to all who'd stand
and listen,
"I want these outlaws dead and gone."

There was someone cruel and angry
A local sheriff of the town.
In Nottingham he sat and plotted
To have the fugitives put down.

He called a contest,
one of archery
That Robin wanted to attend.
When he won with ease and talent
He came nearly to his end.

After fighting with much fury
He was captured, bound, and chained.
In a dungeon he lay bleeding.
Had his life been all in vain?

Little John and Much the Miller
Rode through the gateway
in disguise
Into town to see the Sheriff
And with ease deceived his eyes.

"We have a message from His
Highness:
Hang the traitor well and high.
Take us to identify him."
And the two were taken nigh.

Facing Robin through the
iron bars
Little John gave him a wink.
The Merrymen engaged in battle
Before the guards could really think.

They led Robin through the gateway
With their henchmen waiting there.
Fighting hard and in great danger
They fled back towards their lair.

Sir Guy of Gisborne was a villain.
Folk were terrified and ran.
It was said he murdered children.
He was the Sherrif's righthand man.

With Robin free, he boiled with fury.
Marion had been the bride he bought.
The outlaw's neck upon the scaffold
Was the cruel revenge he sought.

He hunted Robin in the forest
Through the greenwood dark
and dim
'Til face to face he found the
outlaw
With the aim of killing him.

With swords drawn, they fought
for hours
Then they used their bows instead.
Robin was a brilliant bowman.
Guy of Gisborne soon lay dead.

Good King Richard back in England
Hearing of the outlaws bold
Determined to find out himself
The truth of stories he'd been told.

Dressed in monk's clothes like an abbot
He traveled to a forest glade
Became surrounded by the outlaws
But he seemed quite unafraid.

"Come, good abbot, join our supper,"

Said the leader bold and true.

"My good friends, are you the King's men?"

Asked the abbot, though he knew.

"Yes, we are, sir," said brave Robin.

Richard's cowl fell off his head.

They knelt and offered him their homage.

They would follow where he led.

ROBIN'S DEATH

The years that passed in
Richard's service
Were most happy and content
'Til the King's death brought
misfortune.
Back to Sherwood they all went.

Bad King John had plunged the
country
Into discontent and war.
Robin's wife had died in battle.
His sad heart could take no more.

An old wound had troubled Robin
And with no wife there at his side
An evil abbess offered treatment.
'Twas from poison that he died.

As his life went from his body
He drew back his bow to cry,
"Bury me where falls this arrow
Where it lands, there I must lie."

In the forest dark and hidden
Died the hero, Robin Hood
Buried 'neath an aging oak tree
Just a memory of good.

And the stories of brave Robin
With his loyal and merry band
And the deeds they did for justice
Have endured throughout the land.